My First Book about Ladybugs

Amazing Animal Books
Children's Picture Books
By Molly Davidson

Mendon Cottage Books

JD-Biz Publishing

Read More Amazing Animal Books

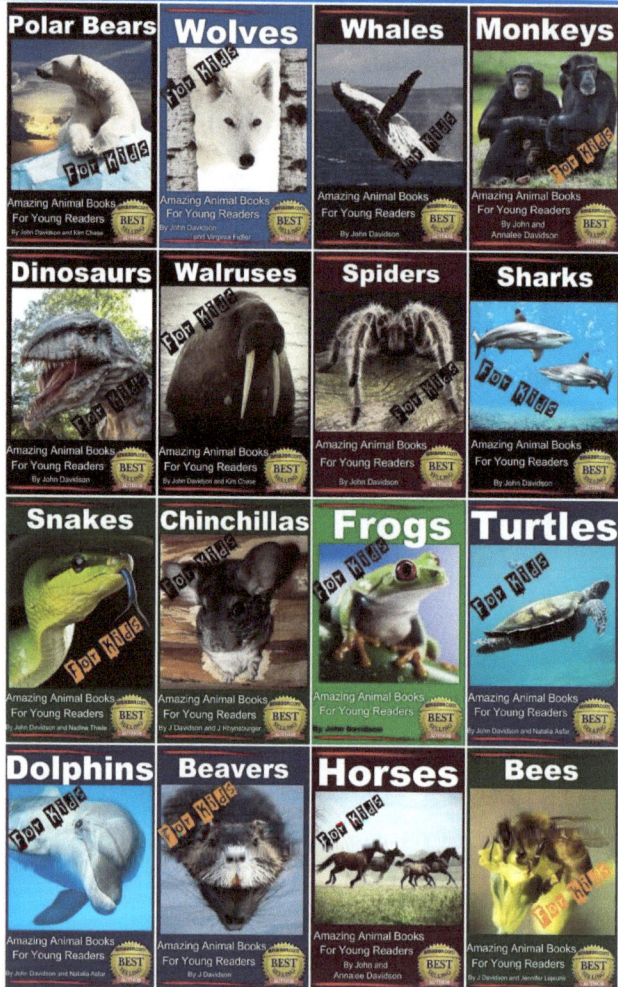

Purchase at Amazon.com
Download Free Books!
http://MendonCottageBooks.com

Table of Contents

Introduction

Ladybugs have three body segments, several eyes, 6 legs, and antennae.

They are helpful creatures in the garden, field, and forest. They eat the harmful insects that destroy plants, crops, and trees.

What are ladybugs?

A ladybug is actually not a bug it's a beetle.

In Britain, they are called lady beetles, which came from a Latin word meaning little sphere (a sphere is a ball shape).

Lady bugs make a little chattering sound, but humans cannot hear it.

Ladybugs start as a little yellow egg, then change into larvae, then pupa, and last a lady bug; this takes about 4 weeks.

Ladybugs live for only about 1 to 2 years.

As a ladybug grows up, her shell gets harder and the color gets darker.

What a ladybug looks like

Ladybugs are about the size of a pencil eraser.

They have 2 pairs of wings; the hard outer wings, these are used for protection, and the soft inner wings are used for flying.

They cannot see in color, just black and white.

A ladybugs head is thin and flat; it has on it a mouth, eyes, and antennas.

A ladybugs antenna is used to help it steer, it can sense things that the ladybug needs to climb over or avoid.

Ladybugs wings are exact mirror images of each other.

Ladybugs in Love

Ladybugs will mate in the springtime.

The girl will lay hundreds of teeny tiny yellow eggs, on a leaf or a tree trunk.

The eggs take about 4 - 6 days to hatch, and the eggs that hatch first, usually eat the other eggs, as their first meal.

After hatching they are larvae, then pupa, and finally a soft ladybug (remember their wings get harder as they get older).

How to spot different types of ladybugs

They can be many colors, not just red, like gray, white, green, brown, or even orange.

They can be one solid color or a mix; some have spots some do not.

Ladybugs are bright colors, because they look poisonous to birds that may try to eat them.

Girl ladybugs are bigger than the boys.

There are over 400 species of ladybugs just in North America; and over 5,000 in the World!

Ladybugs eat smaller insects, and if they are really hungry, they will suck nectar from flowers.

Ladybugs are Helpful

They like to eat soft-bodied pests like aphids, which destroy farmer's crops.

Aphids are green, black, or white, and eat the life right out of plants and trees,

Gardeners will actually buy ladybugs to put in their garden to help with pests.

Ladybugs also each larvae, with destroys the roots of crops, making them unable to grow.

In 2013, the Minnesota Mall of America, let 72,000 ladybugs go inside, this was to help kill all the pests eating the bushes and plants in the mall.

Why do ladybugs smell when they are crushed?

Ladybugs will ooze a sticky, horrible smelling, yellow, bitter liquid from their joints when they get crushed by accident or when they feel threatened.

This is how they defend themselves from predators; it makes them look gross and not wanted.

How to get rid of ladybugs

Ladybugs like to be warm, so in the fall, when the weather gets colder, they may try to sneak into your house for warmth.

You may also see them on the southwest side of your house or a tree; this is where they can get the most sun.

Sweeping up ladybugs doesn't work, because their shells are slippery and the yellow liquid can stain floors.

An easy way to get rid of them is just to vacuum them up.

When you are emptying your vacuum canister, you can catch the ladybugs in a paper towel, and release them outside far from your home.

If they become a big problem, you can call a pest control company.

Lastly, be sure your doors and windows are sealed tight, and never left open, this is help keep bugs (of all kinds) out of your house.

How did the ladybug get her name?

In the middle ages, farmers prayed to Lady Mary for ladybugs to come save their crops.

Many ladybugs came and the farmers' crops were saved.

Lady Mary was usually painted wearing a red coat which looked like the ladybugs shell.

So the ladybug became known as the ladybug, because of Lady Mary.

Some other names are God's cow, lady clock, lady cow, and lady fly.

Ladybugs in the farming field

Farmers need to guard their crops again predators, and ladybugs are a great way of doing this.

Ladybugs eat aphids and other plant eating pests.

Some farmers will plant flowers next to their food crops to help attract ladybugs, so they will come eat their pests.

In California in 1880, thousands of ladybugs were bought and released onto an orchard filled with lemon and orange trees.

The trees were all dying and were infected.

Two years after releasing the ladybugs the trees were all healthy and produced more fruit than ever before.

Ladybugs and tree diseases of the forest

Diseased bugs eat trees and leaves, caused trees to die.

If there are too many of these bugs, they can kill whole forests.

Ladybugs like to eat these kinds of bugs also, helping to save the tree.

Ladybugs are so helpful in saving farmers' crops and our beautiful forests.

Ladybugs around the World and in your backyard

Ladybugs live all over the World, except in Antarctica, it is too cold for them.

If you want to have ladybugs in your yard, you should have flowers and plenty of water.

You can ask a local gardening store for flowers that grow where you live, especially ones that attract ladybugs.

To study a ladybug, they are easy to catch.

The best time to catch them is in the spring because there are many of them roaming around.

You can just nudge a ladybug off a leaf into a plastic container, old pill bottle, or glass jar.

To keep your ladybug from flying away, you can over the top with a bug net.

Your ladybug will also like if you cut off a few leaves and placed them in the container.

Seasons for ladybugs

Ladybugs just find a place to relax in the winter, they don't fly around.

In the spring, when it gets warm, ladybugs start to come out and find mate.

They will then lay their eggs, and go look for food for themselves.

Ladybugs may migrate to the mountains in the summer.

As ladybugs fly, the wind pushes them, since they are so small.

Once they reach the mountains, thousands of ladybugs will join together to help keep predator away, and help each other find food.

When the temperature, in the fall, gets below 55°F, they will go rest again until the next spring.

Conclusion

Ladybugs are very helpful insects, and without them, many farmers would not have healthy crops, and many plants and forests would be destroyed.

Nature thanks the ladybug!

Read More Amazing Animal Books

Purchase at Amazon.com

Website http://AmazingAnimalBooks.com

Our books are available at

1. Amazon.com
2. Barnes and Noble
3. Itunes
4. Kobo
5. Smashwords
6. Google Play Books

Download Free Books!
http://MendonCottageBooks.com

Publisher

JD-Biz Corp

P O Box 374

Mendon, Utah 84325

http://www.jd-biz.com/

www.ingramcontent.com/pod-product-compliance
Lightning Source LLC
Chambersburg PA
CBHW050856290526
45792CB00002B/618